Scoular Anderson

TEACHER TAMING

PUFFIN

For Scott L.

PUFFIN BOOKS

Published by the Penguin Group
Penguin Books Ltd, 80 Strand, London WC2R 0RL, England
Penguin Putnam Inc., 375 Hudson Street, New York, New York 10014, USA
Penguin Books Australia Ltd, 250 Camberwell Road,
Camberwell, Victoria 3124, Australia
Penguin Books Canada Ltd, 10 Alcorn Avenue, Toronto, Ontario, Canada M4V 3B2
Penguin Books India (P) Ltd, 11 Community Centre, Panchsheel Park,
New Delhi – 110 017, India
Penguin Books (NZ) Ltd, Cnr Rosedale and Airborne Roads,
Albany, Auckland, New Zealand
Penguin Books (South Africa) (Pty) Ltd, 24 Sturdee Avenue,
Rosebank 2196, South Africa

Penguin Books Ltd, Registered Offices: 80 Strand, London WC2R 0RL, England

www.penguin.com

First published 2003
1

Set in Lemonade Regular

Made and printed in England by Clays Ltd, St Ives plc

British Library Cataloguing in Publication Data
A CIP catalogue record for this book is available from the British Library

ISBN 0–141–31664–0

Scoular And
School of Art. H
University and as a
in central Scotland. He
for children and adults a
in his native Argyllshire in the
works freelance.

Contents

Hello, I'm your supply teacher.

What Is Teacher Taming?

So exactly what is teacher taming
and how will it help YOU?

This book won't teach you how to tame your teacher the way a lion tamer tames lions.

Once you've read the book, you won't be able to boss your teacher about like you do with your little brother.

You won't be able to stop your teacher giving you homework.

And you won't get them to dance around the playground with you. (Maybe that's a good thing!)

The bad news is that this sort of teacher taming is impossible. Let's face it, your teacher always arrives in school armed to the teeth and ready to do battle...

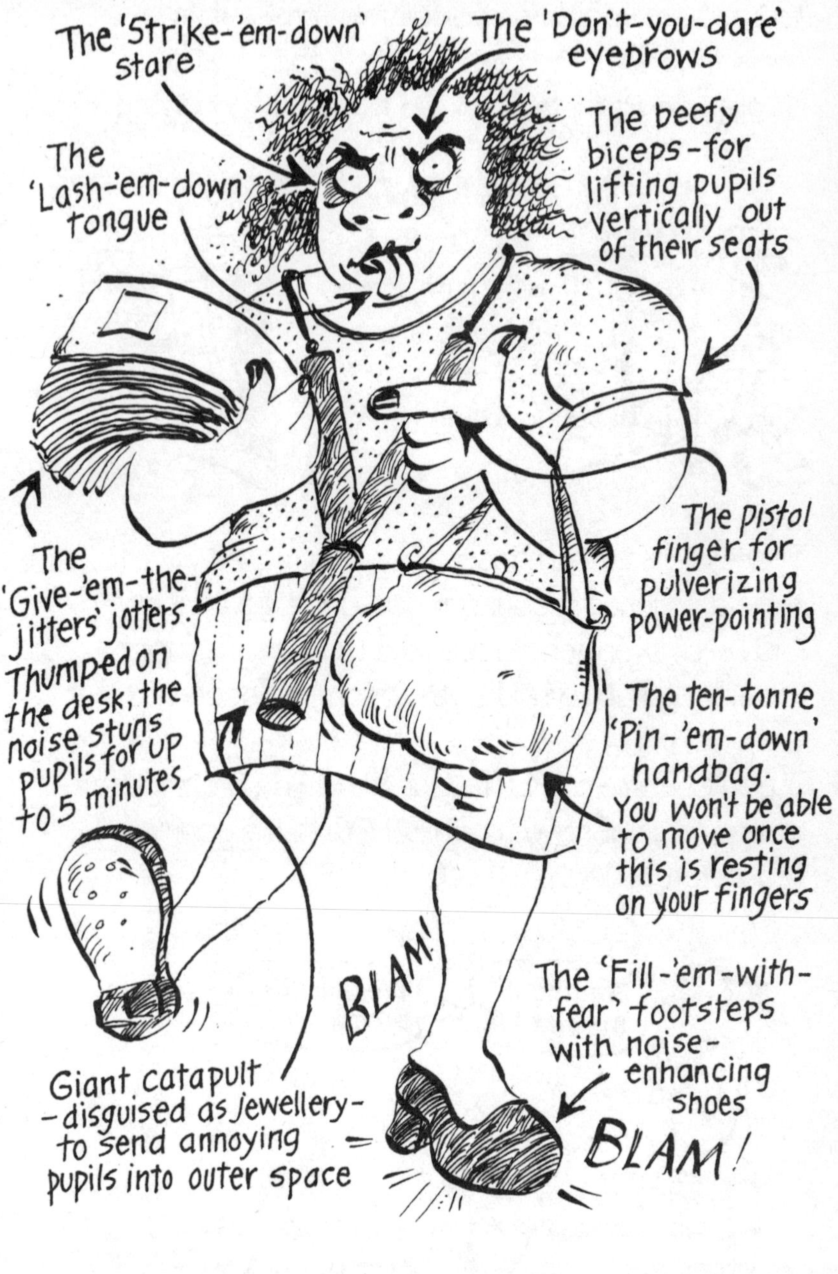
The 'Strike-'em-down' stare
The 'Don't-you-dare' eyebrows
The 'Lash-'em-down' tongue
The beefy biceps – for lifting pupils vertically out of their seats
The 'Give-'em-the-jitters' jotters. Thumped on the desk, the noise stuns pupils for up to 5 minutes
The pistol finger for pulverizing power-pointing
The ten-tonne 'Pin-'em-down' handbag. You won't be able to move once this is resting on your fingers
BLAM!
The 'Fill-'em-with-fear' footsteps with noise-enhancing shoes
Giant catapult – disguised as jewellery – to send annoying pupils into outer space
BLAM!

You're never going to completely tame a fully armed teacher. The good news is that this book is full of handy hints that will help you through the

DANGEROUS DAY

from 9 o'clock to 3 o'clock when untamed teachers are on the warpath.

There is a second reason why you might want to tame a teacher. Because, if you don't, you will be known all over school as a **SPLUT**. (That's short for **S**loppy **P**upil who **L**oves **U**ntamed **T**eachers.)

If you become a **SPLUT** your life will be a complete misery. You will have to do EVERYTHING your teacher tells you.

In fact, a **SPLUT** will quickly become a **SPLUTTER**. (Short for **S**ilent **P**upil who **L**istens to **U**n**T**amed **T**eachers' **E**very **R**ant.)

However, if you use this book and succeed in your taming you will no longer be a **SPLUT** but a **SPLATTT**! (Short for **S**uper **P**upil who **L**earns **A**ll the **T**eacher **T**aming **T**ricks.) You might even become so good at it you will be a **SPLATTT STAR**. (Short for **S**uper **P**upil who **L**earns **A**ll the **T**eacher **T**aming **T**ricks and **S**ends **T**hem **A**way **R**eeling.)

How To Get Started

Why are we starting teacher taming in the middle of a jungle?

We're here to interview Professor Elbert G. Taskpurse who is an expert on watching things.

You must be very, very patient and watch for a long time!
I have been watching gorillas for 25 years.
I know... er... their every move...
I know everything about gorillas and what goes on in their minds.
KISS!
They have got used to me and are now very tame.

We can use Professor Taskpurse's watching method to help us with our teacher taming. Before you can tame a teacher you have to get to know them by 'Teacher Watching'. However, there are a few problems with the Professor's method.

PROBLEM NUMBER 1

Teachers aren't anything like gorillas, of course. If you look at these pictures of a group of gorillas and a group of teachers you will see that they are not the same IN ANY WAY.

(Unfortunately, the teachers won't allow this picture to be seen.)

PROBLEM NUMBER 2

If you're like Professor Taskpurse and watch your teacher for twenty-five years to find out about them, you will eventually be about thirty-three years old and your teacher will be very, very old.

PROBLEM NUMBER 3

How do you watch the teacher without the teacher watching you?

Teacher Watching Kit

Here is Samantha Topkatt on her way to school. (Can you spot the teacher, by the way?)

Why is Samantha's schoolbag so heavy? She's going to do some serious teacher watching and prepare herself for teacher taming. She's carrying a complete **Teach-U-Watch kit** in her bag.

This is the kind of stuff you need to do some serious teacher watching ...

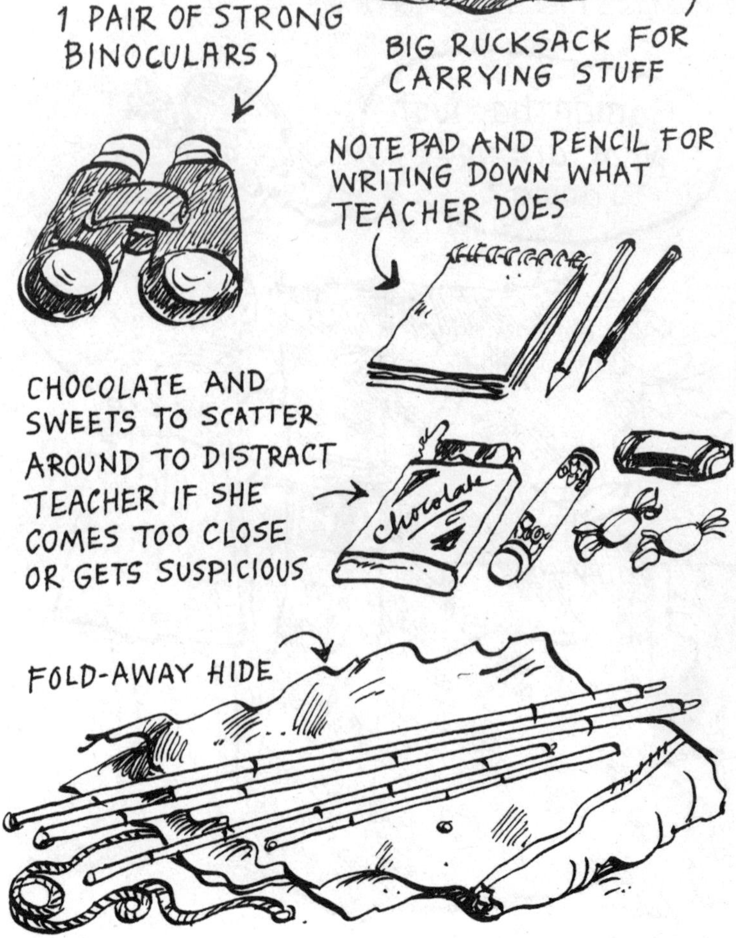

The most important piece of equipment is a hide. Bird watchers use one of these. It's usually a tent camouflaged with bits of twigs and leaves. The bird watchers crawl inside the hide and watch the birds without the birds watching them.

However, your teacher might get suspicious if you take a hide into the classroom.

It's better to make a hide out of other things in the classroom – e.g. jotters, schoolbags, other pupils etc.

The SOB Gauge

The aim of teacher watching is to discover some of their little quirks. Teacher quirks come in three sizes: **S**illy, **O**dd and **B**izarre. This is known as the **SOB Gauge**. Teachers' little quirks will make you either sob with laughter or sob with fear. As an example, look at these two objects:

And here are the three SOBs:

1 Teacher always forgets to water the plant.

SOB level: plain silly

2 Teacher often talks to plant.

SOB level: slightly odd

3 Teacher pulls the petals off flowers one by one while cackling to herself.

SOB level: definitely bizarre

Once you have identified a quirk and its SOB level you can use this information to teacher tame.

Teacher Taming Method 1
Quick Tricks

Once you have learnt to watch your teacher closely and can identify their quirks, you can start teacher taming.

IMPORTANT WARNING!

To begin with, keep things simple. Avoid fancy, complicated teacher taming methods.

A beginner who tries to tame their teacher with a mobile phone, a feather duster, a pineapple and a large wig is bound to fail. They will become known throughout the school as a **FOOTTBAL**. (Short for Failure Of Over-confident Teacher Taming By Ambitious Learner.)

Begin with Teacher Taming Method 1 – using simple tricks to confuse, muddle, surprise or (if everything else fails) flatter your teacher into being tamed.

The four rules of Teacher Taming

1 Choose your victim – sorry, teacher – and do some serious teacher watching.

2 Identify their quirks and their SOB level.

3 Using the facts you have gathered, begin teacher taming.

4 Sit back and enjoy the results.

On the next page is a short guide to get you started on some simple teacher taming tricks.

1
gulp!
Yoo-hoo!
IF THERE'S A SPIDER IN THE ROOM, WATCH YOUR TEACHER CAREFULLY TO SEE IF SHE TWITCHES.
SOB = SILLY
TEACHER TAME BY BEING AS SPIDERY AS YOU CAN - SHE WON'T DARE BOTHER YOU!
2
TEACHER MAKES STRANGE THREATS
SOB = ODD
If anyone gets out of their seat again, the crocodiles will get them!
TWO CAN PLAY AT THAT GAME...
Help! Help!
The crocodiles are after us!
3
TEACHER IS REALLY NEAT AND TIDY.
SOB = ODD
MESS UP HIS DESK - HE'LL BE SO UPSET HE'LL CANCEL LESSONS.
Aargh!

4
EVERY DAY, TEACHER ARRIVES BY BIKE, PARKS IT AND GIVES IT A LITTLE DUST.
SOB = BIZARRE
HIDE BIKE AT THE BACK OF SCHOOL. PLACE OLD BIKE WHEEL UNDER HEAD TEACHER'S CAR. (SCATTER A FEW NUTS AND BOLTS AROUND FOR EXTRA EFFECT.)
Aaargh! MY BIKE!
5
TEACHER WEARS LOTS OF MAKE-UP AND GLITTERY JEWELLERY
SOB = SILLY
MAKE SURE YOUR PAINTINGS AND COLLAGES ARE FULL OF BRIGHT, GLITTERY THINGS - SHE'LL MELT WITH DELIGHT.
HOW LOVELY!

The History Of Teacher Taming
The Stone Age

Teacher taming has been practised for thousands of years and you can pick up some very handy hints by looking at how teachers were tamed in the past. Here is our very first teacher taming history section.

The **GOOD** thing about the Stone Age was there were no schools and no teachers. The **BAD** thing about the Stone Age was just about everyone wanted to teach you something about everything.

Your mum, grannies, big sisters etc, would have taught you how to scrape animal skins for making clothes.

Your dad, uncles, grandpas, big brothers etc, would have taught you how to hunt.

Even the thing you were hunting (dinner) would teach you not to miss with your arrow.

Since there were a lot of teachers to tame, it was best to tame them all in one go. One way was to wait until they were all sitting together (e.g. story time). Next, you found a very big animal (e.g. mammoth) ...

... or one with lots of spikes on its face (e.g. wart hog).

You annoyed the animal a little bit ...

... then you ran.

You ran in the direction of the teachers and just at the last minute you swerved out of the way.

Important Things You Should Know About Teachers

Just because you have been introduced to the most basic of the teacher taming methods, does that mean you are on your way to becoming a SPLATTT STAR?

Unfortunately, it's not as easy as that. If a teacher gets suspicious that you are up to something, you may well find yourself rising vertically out of your seat ...

... or even heading for outer space.

To avoid detection there are some important things you should know about your teacher.

You must beware of teachers' eyes, ears, noses and mouths – in other words, the DANGEROUS HEAD WEAPONS.

Teachers' Eyes

It's very difficult to do anything in a classroom without a teacher noticing. This is because teachers have very special eyes. Teachers' eyes are a cross between a vulture's and a chameleon's.

The vulture has a bit in the middle of its eye which is like a telescope. The vulture can spot things, even when it's flying high in the sky.

The chameleon can swivel its eyes in all directions so that one eye can look to the left while the other eye is looking to the right.

This is why teachers never miss a thing. Their eyes are like security cameras, always patrolling the room or the corridor.

On the next page you'll see what a teacher sees in the classroom. You would have to look around at these things, one after another. The teacher can see all of them AT THE SAME TIME.

SHE SEES KEVIN'S HAND STRETCHING OUT TO BORROW ZEB'S PEN (WITHOUT PERMISSION)...
...SHE SEES ROBBIE PICKING HIS NOSE...
... AND A FLY WALKING ACROSS THE CEILING...
...SHE CAN TELL THAT MELANIE HASN'T HAD BREAKFAST...
CRISPS
... AND SHE CAN TELL WHAT TIME IT IS BECAUSE SHE CAN SEE DAVID'S WATCH EVEN THOUGH HE'S RIGHT AT THE BACK OF THE CLASS...
TEACHER VISION

TO THE LEFT, TRACY'S PAINTING HAS JUST COME OFF THE WALL...
... AND THROUGH THE WINDOW TO THE RIGHT, SHE CAN SEE THOMAS ARRIVING LATE...
... BUT TEACHER VISION CAN ZOOM IN AND SEE THAT THAT THOMAS HAS NITS IN HIS HAIR...
... AND SHE CAN TELL THAT MICHAEL HAS JUST STUCK OUT HIS TONGUE...
... BECAUSE TEACHERS HAVE A SPECIAL EXTRA PAIR OF EYES, LIKE REVERSING LIGHTS, IN THE BACK OF THEIR HEADS.
Get on with your work, Michael!
WHOOSH!

Taming a teacher's eyesight is tricky. You could try giving her a pair of very dark sunglasses and persuade her to wear them.

There is another thing about teachers' eyesight you must be careful about. A Gorgon was a creature who turned people to stone just by looking at them. Well, teachers can do something very similar.

It's called the LOOK, or the **VRAPS**. This is short for **V**ision that **R**educes **A**wkward **P**upils to **S**ogginess. If you misbehave, you'll feel the **VRAPS** sizzling towards you across the classroom.

It's very difficult to tame these deadly rays. If you're quick, you could duck.

You could deflect the rays with a small mirror if you have one handy.

If you aim right, you could give your teacher a taste of her own medicine ...

Teachers' Ears

Teachers also have special ears and you must be very careful what you say in class. This is because, when a normal person comes into a noisy room, they will just hear an awful din ...

But when a teacher comes into a noisy room she will hear ALL the conversations at the same time and very loud.

Teachers have a weapon in their ears which is almost as lethal as the VRAPS. It's called the WHISPER DISH.

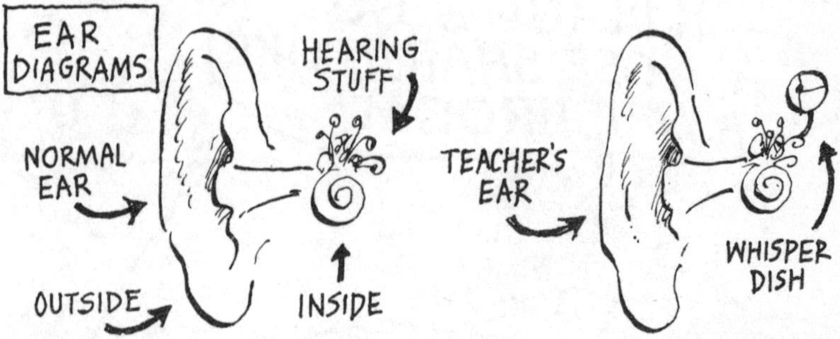

The Whisper Dish is like a satellite dish and it can pick up the smallest sounds – e.g. a teacher can hear a leaf drop off a plant at the back of the room.

A teacher can hear a spider walking past under the floorboards.

So when you're whispering to your pal, it actually sounds like this to a teacher.

The Whisper Dish is a very powerful weapon and very difficult to avoid. You could learn to speak a foreign language – like Russian – so your teacher wouldn't understand what you were saying.

You could give her a pair of ear muffs though it might not be easy to persuade her to wear them.

You could try and stuff some cotton wool into her ears but unless you are James Bond, this will be very difficult.

Teachers' Voices

There is one more weapon a teacher has – that is her voice. Sounds are measured in decibels, e.g. a whisper is 20 decibels.

When a teacher is talking to you in class her voice will be as loud as leaves rustling in a gentle breeze. (30 Decibels)

However, teachers have a special gadget in their lungs called the BELLOW BOOSTER. They use it when they want to shout loudly (70 decibels) or very loudly (90 decibels).

Using the Bellow Booster at full strength, a teacher can shout as loud as 140 decibels. The sound will be as loud as if you were standing next to a jet aircraft as it takes off.

You could try taming a noisy teacher with a really chewy toffee...

...or make up a snack with chillies and loads of pepper.

Now you know how to deactivate your teacher's Head Weapons and can move on to more complex methods of teacher taming.

The History Of Teacher Taming
The Ancient Egyptians

The Ancient Egyptians didn't use writing like ours. They used pictures called hieroglyphs. These were painted on walls or carved out of stone. This meant homework took a long, long time.

There were only two other subjects in Egyptian schools. They were known as maths and mums.

Maths was a bit boring because the only shapes they studied were pyramids. Look at these examples of Egyptian homework:

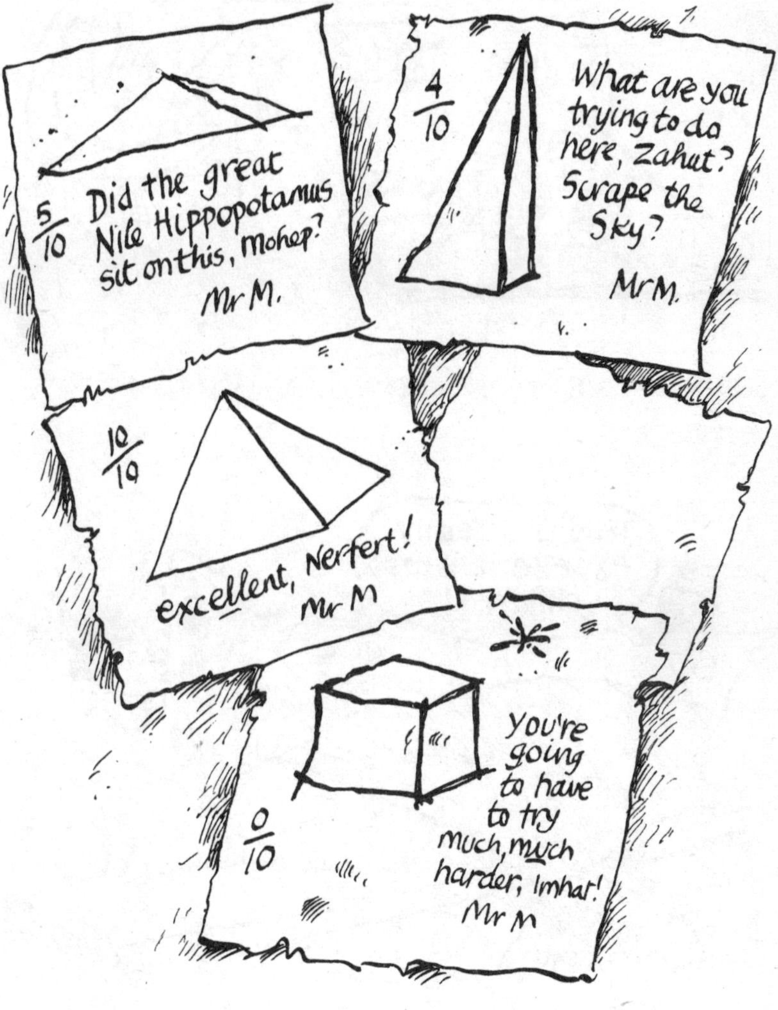

Mums is short for mummy-wrapping. Pupils usually started by wrapping a brick or their lunch-time sandwiches.

Sometimes pupils were allowed to wrap their teachers.

Of course, they had to remember to unwrap their teacher again or they might be buried right in the middle of a huge pyramid by mistake. That was known as Egyptian teacher taming.

Teacher Taming Method 2
Teachers' Favourite Things

While you are teacher watching, it is very important to try and find out your teacher's favourite things. You can use the information in two ways.

THE KIND WAY If a teacher says she really likes chocolate, then you can make sure she gets lots of chocolate at special times (e.g. Christmas, end-of-term, school outings, her birthday, everyone's birthday, Friday afternoons etc). This will keep your teacher sweet and happy – and a happy teacher is a tame teacher.

THE CRUEL WAY Find out what your teacher really likes then do all you can to stop her getting it (e.g. a mug of coffee). So, just as the bell goes for playtime you can ...

... put up your hand to ask a question ...

... lose something important ...

... fidget in the line ...

... or faint loudly.

The longer the teacher has to wait for her coffee the less capable of teaching (and hassling you) she will be. She will be successfully tamed!

If you don't do your teacher-watching research properly, the 'favourite things' method can easily go wrong. Here are three examples of where teacher taming had unexpected results.

Example One

Teacher: Mr Dissko

School: Lower Forklifte School

Favourite Things: walking the dog, spaghetti, horses

When he said 'horses', Mr Dissko meant he liked watching horse racing on the telly.

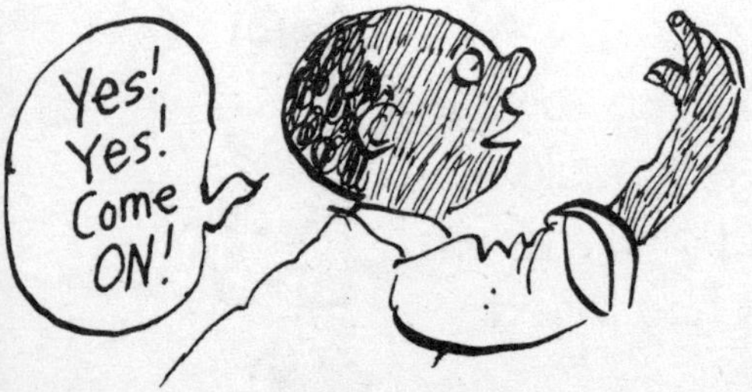

He was actually terrified of real horses ...

...so when Jane brought her pony Carmen into school as a surprise treat for Mr Dissko, he was so frightened he almost hid under his desk.

Unfortunately, Carmen took a liking to Mr Dissko, especially his tie.

Mr Dissko could never watch horses on telly again and, without his favourite hobby, he became a grumpy teacher who gave double homework every lesson.

Example Two

Teacher: Miss Shelflyffe
School: Mouldyhill School
Favourite Things:
crunchy green apples,
holidays in the sun, rowing

Her class thought the last thing on the list was a bit strange but they arranged a taming session anyway. An aunty of one of the pupils was an actor so they got her to come and start a row with Miss Shelflyffe.

As rows went, it was a good row ...

... it became a really excellent row ...

... in fact, it went right off the top of the rowometer.

Then one of the pupils noticed a sticker on Miss Shelflyffe's car window.

It wasn't rowing that Miss Shelflyffe liked it was ... er ... rowing.

The row made Miss Shelflyffe so angry, for the next week, every time a pupil put their hand up in class Miss Shelflyffe started an argument with them.

Example Three

Teacher: Mrs Hamstrung
School: Bogwood Street School
Favourite Things: flowers in vases, freshly baked scones, dance

When she wrote 'dance' Mrs Hamstrung really meant going to see this kind of dance ...

... but her pupils got it wrong.

One of her pupils had a cousin who was in the Lively Lizards Limbo Line-up. The Line-up came to surprise Mrs Hamstrung.

After her dance workout, Mrs Hamstrung was so exhausted she fell asleep at her desk and didn't wake up until the cleaners prodded her with a mop.

Things really backfired when Mrs Hamstrung decided she really liked limbo dancing. Now she makes her pupils limbo dance for ten minutes first thing every morning to wake them up.

The History Of Teacher Taming
The Romans

The *Romans* were very keen on keeping fit. Teachers made pupils do a lot of workouts.

The Romans were also very keen on marching. Pupils were expected to walk up and down for hours.

After that, teachers took their pupils to the baths. That might sound quite nice but plunging into a really hot bath ...

... followed by a cold bath was a bit of a shock.

However, there was one easy way to tame your teacher in Roman times that never failed. First, you looked for an ad for new gladiators.

You then sent away for an application form and filled it in.

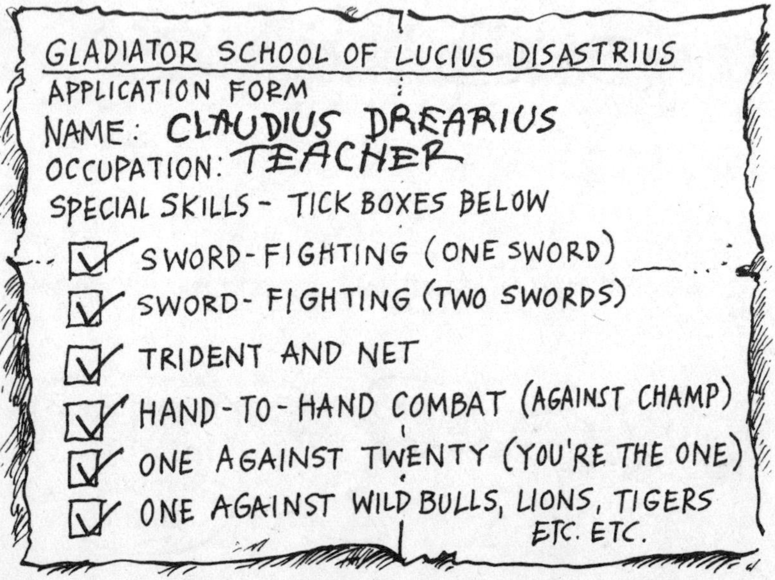

You sent off the form and ...

You then made sure you had a good front-row seat in the arena.

Teacher Taming Method 3
The Secrets Of The Staffroom

Most of the time your teachers are with you in the classroom. But sometimes they escape to the staffroom. You may think of the staffroom as a forbidden zone, impossible to enter. But teachers can be tamed here, too. It's a very mysterious place. Usually you only get a quick glimpse inside when the door opens. But now we can exclusively reveal the secrets of the staffroom, which will help you with your teacher taming.

Sometimes you may have to go and speak to a teacher in the staffroom. The door can look quite scary. The noise behind it is even scarier.

You will have to knock on the door. Which knock do you think you should use?

If you use knock number 1, no one will hear you.

If you use knock number 2, you will probably get this reaction.

If you use knock number 4, this will happen.

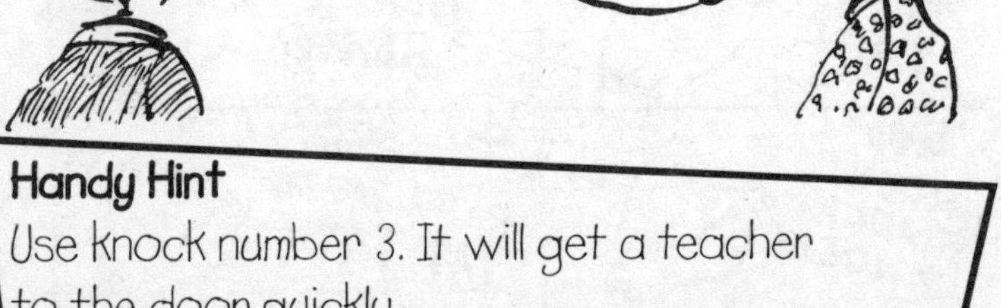

Handy Hint

Use knock number 3. It will get a teacher to the door quickly.

If you ever get into a staffroom the first thing you will see is *MUGS*.

There will be herds of mugs in the sink.

There will be flocks of mugs on the tables ...

... and on the chairs.

Teachers have a strange obsession with mugs and just cannot get enough of them.

The Tea-Break Ritual

There is a lot of bizarre behaviour in the staffroom but the strangest sights can be seen during the 'Tea-Break Ritual'.

At 10.30 precisely, the bell for playtime goes off. At 10.31 precisely, the teachers arrive at the staffroom in an orderly fashion.

At 10.32, the teachers form a neat line with their mugs in front of the boiler.

By 10.34, the teachers have dunked their teabags and swirled their coffee granules in their mugs.

By 10.35 they have adjusted the flavour with milk or sugar.

At 10.36 the teachers sit down in their seats. They like to sit in the same seat every day so if anyone is in the wrong seat there may be a little trouble.

At 10.37 precisely, there is silence in the staffroom as the teachers take their first sip ...

At 10.39 the teachers begin rummaging in their bags for their teacher SNACKS. What teachers eat is a closely guarded secret and readers who faint easily should skip the next few pages.

First come the crisps. There are deafening crunching noises as the teachers gobble their crisps and disgusting slurps as they lick the crumbs from the inside of the packets.

At 10.40 and 30 seconds precisely, the teachers rummage in their bags again. Even though it is only break time they are going to eat their lunch. The teachers stuff themselves with tuna sandwiches with green bits (frog's legs?), octopus-flavoured yogurts, chocolate and bacon filled rolls, boiled ostrich eggs, grilled worms ...

... in fact, anything they have grabbed from the fridge as they left home.

At precisely 10.42 some teachers who are still hungry are heating up bits of staffroom carpet in the microwave.

If it's a special day – e.g. the last day of term, or the head teacher is off sick – there will be an extra foody treat. It could be a box of biscuits or a cake, which the teachers eat in an orderly fashion of course.

At 10.45 the bell goes again. The teachers lick their fingers and get ready to go back to their classrooms.

While the teachers are doing all this eating in the staffroom, they are usually marking your homework. This explains all the strange marks that appear on your jotter.

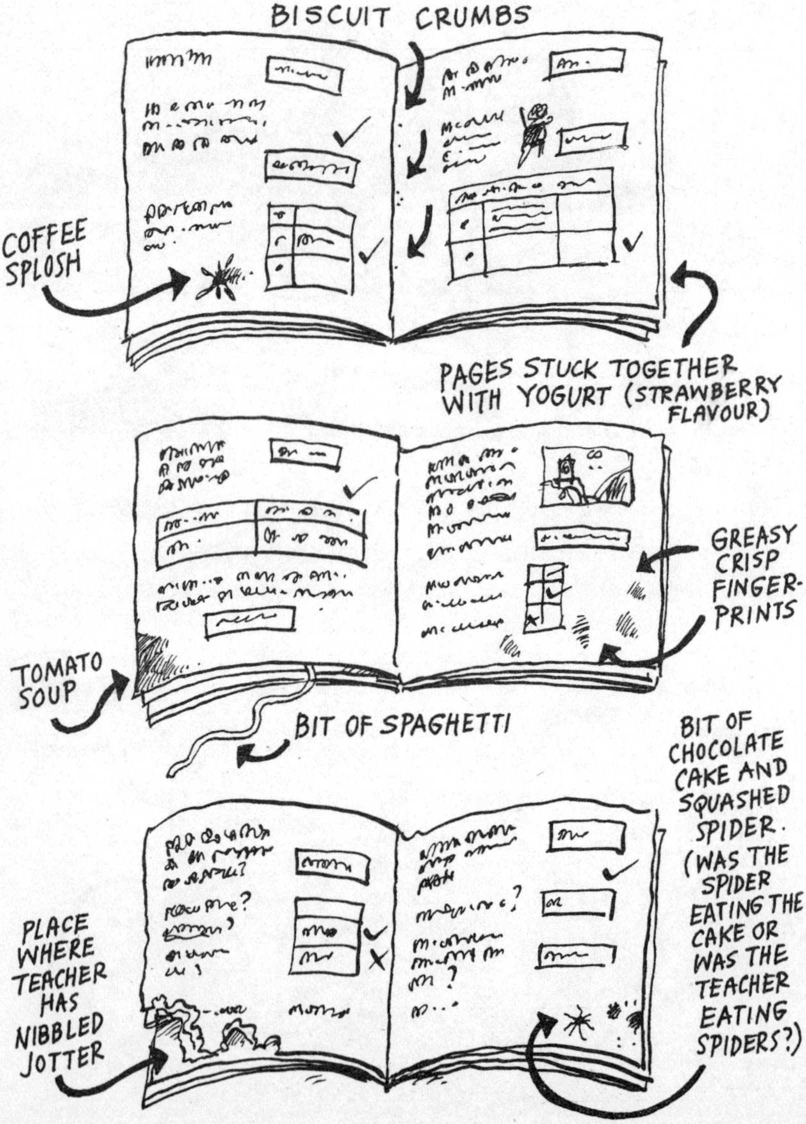

If you're a good detective you'll be able to work out what kind of food your teacher likes. You can then tame your teacher by giving her just the right kind of food as a present.

You could also give her a mug. She probably has fourteen in the staffroom already but teachers can't resist mugs and you will become her star pupil.

During the Tea-Break Ritual is a good time to try some teacher taming. If you want to get right into the staffroom for some 'extreme' teacher taming, you'll have to use a disguise. It would be best if you disguised yourself as a cleaner or an engineer.

Once you are in the staffroom there are lots of tricks you can use to cause a bit of chaos and tame those teachers!

Change the time on the clock.

Move the furniture around.

Staple lots of sheets of paper together and leave big piles on each teacher's seat.

Hide their mugs.

Pin a notice on the boiler.

The History Of Teacher Taming
The Viking Age

During this period of history, teacher taming depended on whether you were a Viking or not. If you weren't a Viking then the Vikings did the teacher taming for you. One minute you were having a reading lesson from your teacher (most probably a monk) ...

The next minute you had visitors.

A visit from the Vikings left your teacher completely tamed and there would be no more school until new books and furniture were made.

If you were a Viking your Viking teachers were probably very fierce. They would give you a hard time when …

… you had to learn to row a Viking ship …

… or use a Viking weapon …

… or carve a Viking message on a stick.

To tame a Viking teacher, you went for the hair. You waited till after they had had a heavy day's plundering and listened to a saga (a very, very long bedtime story) by the fireside.

Then you crept in and cut off all their hair, beards, moustaches, pigtails etc.

A Viking without hair just couldn't be fierce and became tame with embarrassment.

Teacher Taming Method 4
What If Your Teacher Isn't Human?

Let's face it, you could be forgiven for thinking that all teachers are aliens. Just look at how odd they are – the strange shape, wild eyes, the uncool clothes, the way they twitter to one another in a weird language you can't quite hear etc etc.

Can you imagine a teacher doing normal human things like going on a jet-ski on holiday . . .

. . . or singing karaoke on a night out?

Of course not, it's just too horrible to think about.

But, unbelievably, most teachers are human. However, now and then, non-human teachers do end up in your classroom. This part of the book will help you identify non-human teachers and give you some tips on how to deal with their unpredictable behaviour.

How To Tame A Vampire Teacher

First, here are some handy hints on how to tell if your teacher is a vampire.

If your teacher never smiles it *could* just be because she is very grumpy. Or it could be because she is trying to hide her pointy fangs.

Try telling her some funny jokes to make her laugh.

If she laughs, all will be revealed.

Vampires usually sleep during the day and come out at night. If your teacher keeps falling asleep during lessons she's probably a vampire. She's dreaming that she's back home in her comfy coffin.

Vampires can climb up walls. Watch your teacher carefully when she's reaching up high (e.g. pinning up one of your paintings). If her feet leave the chair, be very worried.

It's a well-known fact that vampires hate garlic. Here's an experiment you can try. Get a bulb of garlic and break it into cloves.

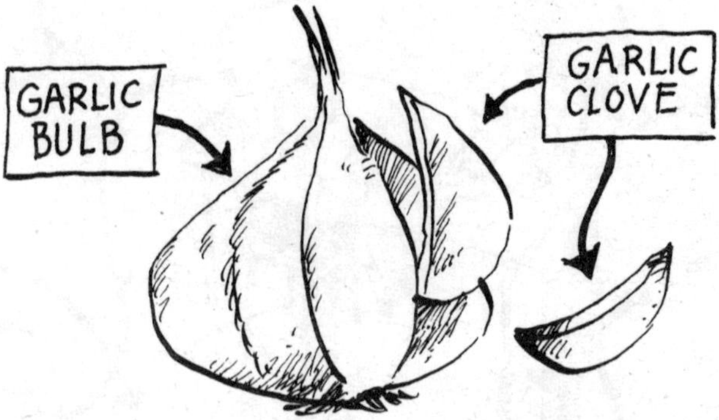

Give some of the pupils in your class garlic cloves to put in their pockets.

Watch how your teacher moves around the class. If she avoids pupils with garlic in their pockets, you'll know she's a VAMPIRE!

PATH OF VAMPIRE TEACHER
PUPILS WITH GARLIC CLOVE MARKED WITH A X
START

Staying Alive

Once you have discovered your teacher is a vampire you must be on your guard at all times. Always wear a scarf round your neck in case your teacher fancies a snack.

Vampires are most active after dark. Take care when you are with the vampire teacher on a school outing after dark.

If you go on a school outing, check out what your teacher is wearing. If she's dressed in a strange cape like this, you can be pretty sure she's just flown in from her vampire castle.

Perhaps the best way to tame a vampire teacher is to become his friend. Let him know that you won't tell the head teacher if he does a favour in return – a little less homework, for example.

How To Tame An Alien Teacher

If a new teacher comes into your class looking like this, you can be sure that he or she is an alien.

However, aliens can be very clever at disguising themselves and may look very human. (**WARNING**: if you are suspicious, never poke or pull at your teacher's skin . If you are right, the skin may come off in your hand and reveal something hideous underneath! If you are wrong, your teacher will be very annoyed.)

If you suspect your teacher is an alien, watch him or her carefully. Their quirks always register as 'bizarre' on the SOB gauge. For example:

If you see your teacher talking to objects – e.g. a television set ...

... or the school piano ...

... then your teacher is probably an alien who has just arrived on earth and is a little confused.

If they think that the tables and chairs are pupils, and the pupils are chairs you definitely have a confused alien as a teacher.

Watching your teacher's eating habits is a good way of checking their alien potential. Offer your teacher a sweet. If she sticks the wrapper in her mouth and drops the sweet in the bin, you may have an alien on your hands.

Follow your teacher when he or she leaves school. If they are alien they may chew leaves when they think no one is looking ...

... or munch slugs.

Of course, if your teacher is an alien she might not drive a car. Watch your teacher carefully when she arrives and leaves school. Here are some alien things to look out for.

1 Does your teacher arrive at school in strange clothes?

2 Does your teacher park her vehicle round the back of the school rather than in the car park?

3 Is your teacher the only person who gets on her bus and is the bus is empty?

4 Does your teacher sometimes arrive in class from the roof, through the window?

5 Does your teacher just suddenly appear as if from nowhere in a beam of light?

Aliens are quite a varied bunch so it's difficult to know what taming method to use. This chart shows a few aliens who have been spotted on Earth.

It may help you to decide if your teacher is an alien and how he or she can be tamed.

...from the planet...	...and the taming method...
SLORSH – damp, damp, rainy, boggy, damp 	THROW HER IN THE NEAREST SWIMMING POOL. POUR WATER DOWN HER NECK. SCOOSH HER WITH WATER PISTOLS. SHE'LL FEEL REALLY AT HOME AND TREAT YOU WELL.
HYDAWAY – Full of dark caves and tunnels where the Timidians spend all their time. 	JUST SAY 'BOO!' – TEACHER INSTANTLY TAMED. 
BADHEYRDAY – If you were a Makeoverian your mum would probably often say: 'Your room's tidy! Mess it up now!'	POUR GLUE OVER HER HEAD. STUFF BITS OF PAPER UP HER NOSTRILS. PAINT HER FACE RED AND GREEN. SHE WILL TREAT THIS AS A GREAT COMPLIMENT AND CANCEL HOMEWORK.
LUNCHANGO 	RUN AWAY VERY, VERY QUICKLY!!

How To Tame A Robot Teacher

If there is a shortage of teachers, your supply teacher may be a robot. Robot teachers can be difficult to spot as they often behave like bored human teachers.

Check the feet. If the teacher has wheels or walks in a funny way, you could have a robotic teacher.

Look out for strange sounds when the teacher talks or makes sudden, peculiar movements.

The chart on the next page shows some more things you should look out for in a robotic teacher.

Teacher speaks in a foreign language. Teacher obviously one of a batch of robots imported from a foreign country.

Teacher starts to malfunction. Stuffs things into cupboards and throws things out of windows. Great fun but you may be next.

Other teachers keep putting their heads round classroom door. Beware! Robotic teacher must have electronic link to other classrooms.

Teacher starts talking gobbledygook. A computer-controlled robotic teacher with a bad virus.

Robot teachers are fairly easy to tame. Here are a few of our favourite methods. They usually have lots of metal in them so a large magnet will keep them out of the way.

Schoolbags laid around the room like a maze will confuse the robotic teacher and send her flying if she dares to leave the safety of her desk.

Bombarding robotic teachers with lots of questions will overload their circuits and make them explode.

If you are lucky, there might be another robot teacher in the school and you could stage robot wars during break time.

The History Of Teacher Taming
The Middle Ages

In the middle ages, children were sent away to someone else's castle to learn things.

Boys stood behind their master's chair at mealtimes and watched them eat. Not a pretty sight.

They would learn to joust by charging at a target with their lance.

Meanwhile, girls were making polite conversation with their mistress in her room while doing a little sewing ...

... or playing music.

A jousting tournament was a good time for the pupils to get their own back. A girl had to help her mistress dress for the tournament. As mirrors weren't very good in those days, the mistress might not notice things weren't as they should be ...

A boy had to help his master put on his armour. If the armour wasn't fastened properly, it would all fall off at the wrong moment.

The Lord and Lady were tamed!

The Ultimate Challenge: Can Head Teachers Be Tamed?

Some people like to climb very high mountains. Other people like to fly hot-air balloons round the world.

Call them brave or call them foolhardy, they do it because they like the ultimate challenge. This is why some pupils dare to try and tame their head teacher.

This is what Professor Taskpurse says on the subject.

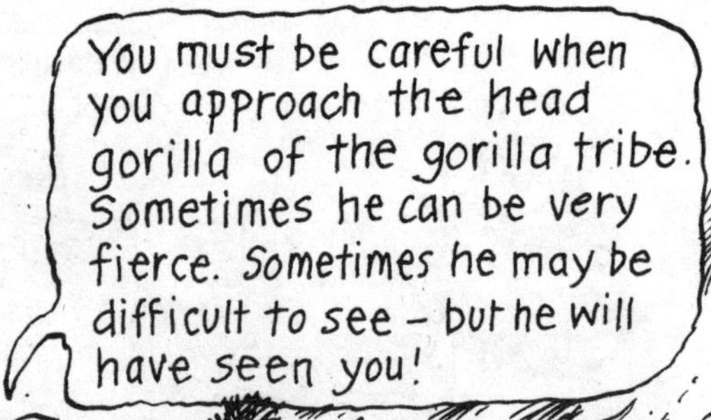

So will you ever get a chance at head teacher taming? First you must be sent to see the head teacher (probably for something naughty). The head is guarded by the school secretary. If it's a big school there will be an office full of guards.

Besides guarding the head teacher, the secretaries are usually in charge of dinner money, lost property and the first-aid box.

While you are waiting to see the head teacher, the secretaries will probably give you extra dinner money, sticking plasters and something to wear from the lost property box.

If you survive the school secretaries and get as far as the head's office, there are still more obstacles to overcome.

1 The head teacher is in but is too busy and can't see you. In that case you may wait outside the office for hours or days or even years.

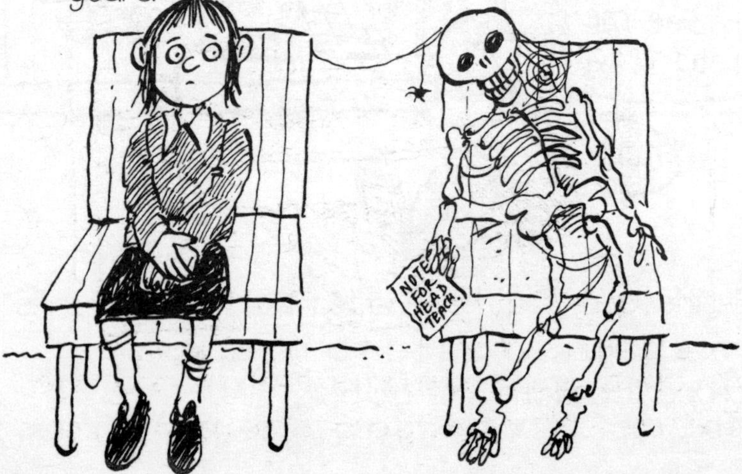

2 The head teacher is out and can't see you. You will have to wait (for hours, days or years) or risk passing the school secretaries again.

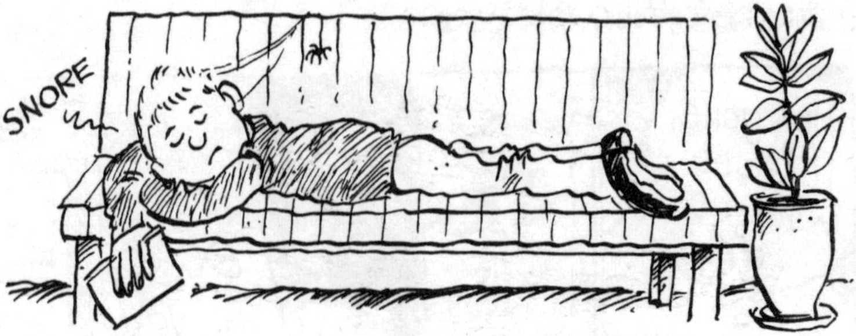

3 You are told that the head teacher will see you but the office is empty. There's no chance of taming and so you leave the forbidden book your teacher said you shouldn't be reading on the head teacher's desk.

As you can see, head teacher taming is impossible! They are far too crafty and try to never let pupils see them. Plus they have another advantage ... Two seconds after you've gone, the head teacher will jump out of a cupboard or leap down from the ceiling and find what you've left...